D0581924

LAUGH
on the LOO
Parragon
Bath • New York • Cologne • Melbourne • Delhi
Hong Kong • Shenzhen • Singapore • Amsterdam

"Never lose an opportunity for pumpship."

*Duke of Wellington*

If you are sitting comfortably, then let us begin. To help you get things moving, here are some top toilet tales – feel free to crack up at your convenience.

# Prime Minister's Questions

The Prime Minister was heading into Number 10 Downing Street on a snowy day. He couldn't fail to miss that just outside his front door, someone had urinated the phrase "The PM is a moron".

Horrified, he demanded his head of security look into who did it.

A couple of days later, the head of security reported back. "Sir, we've run some tests. The urine definitely belongs to the Leader of the Opposition."

"I thought as much," said the PM.

"And," continued the head of security, "the handwriting belongs to your wife."

***

WHAT IS BROWN AND SOUNDS LIKE A BELL?

DUNG!

***

One night, a wife is up late waiting for her husband to come home. "Where have you been?" she asks as he walks in the door, clearly drunk.

"Darling, you wouldn't believe it. I went to this amazing pub. It had gold ashtrays, gold stools, gold cups, and even gold toilets," he replies. Realising it isn't worth talking any further with him in that state, she goes to bed.

The next day she finds a business card for "The Golden Pub" in her husband's pocket. She gives them a call – "Hello, is this the Golden Pub?"

"Yes, madam," comes the reply.

"Right. I need to see if my husband was talking any sense. Do you have golden ashtrays?"

"Yes."

"Do you have golden stools?"

"Yes."

"Do you have golden cups?"

"Yes."

"Do you have golden toilets?"

There is a pause on the phone, then a couple of seconds later she hears the man shout, "Oi, Dave. I think we've found the bloke who crapped in your tuba."

## Over My Head

Two brothers were in the garden having a peeing contest, trying to aim as high up the wall as possible.

Mum appeared and shouted at them for messing up the side of the house. The boys ran off and bumped into their father. He asked them what was going on, so they told him about their contest.

Dad asked, "What did your mother do when she found you?"

"She hit the roof," replied the boys.

"Blimey," said Dad, "did she win?"

## **** THE SURVEY SAID ****

I recently found out that when using the urinal 33% of men hold their "little man" with their left hand and 67% use their right.

89% wanted to know why I was watching them pee.

# Top Farty COUNTDOWN

## A PLAYLIST TO HELP YOU THROUGH EVERY STAGE OF YOUR NEXT VISIT

### SENSING TROUBLE

Black Eyed Peas - I Gotta Feeling
Dizzee Rascal - Fix up, Look Sharp
Europe - Final Countdown
Moody Blues - Go Now

### IT'S NOT MOVING

The Beatles - Help!
Stevie Wonder - Uptight
Salt n Pepa - Push It
Engelbert Humperdinck - Please Release Me, Let Me Go

### IN FULL FLOW

The Birthday Party - Release the Bats
Betty Boo - Doin' the Do
Queen - Another One Bites the Dust
Rolling Stones - Satisfaction

## AND WE'RE DONE

Johnny Cash - Ring of Fire
James Brown - Get Up Offa That Thing
Smiths - This Charming Man

## SOME PARP MUSIC

Thunderclap Newman - Something in the Air
Scorpions - Wind of Change
Dionne Warwick - Walk On By

## FACING THE PORCELAIN

Soundgarden - Burden In My Hand
Princess - Say I'm Your Number One
Police - Don't Stand So Close To Me
Christie - Yellow River

## ON REPEAT

Britney Spears - Oops! I Did It Again

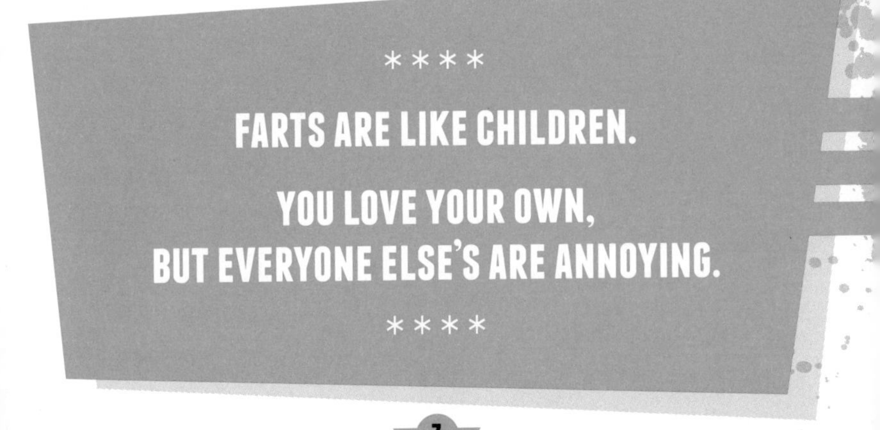

****

FARTS ARE LIKE CHILDREN.

YOU LOVE YOUR OWN,
BUT EVERYONE ELSE'S ARE ANNOYING.

****

## HOW MANY MEN DOES IT TAKE TO CHANGE A ROLL OF TOILET PAPER?

## NO ONE KNOWS... IT'S NEVER BEEN DONE.

A teacher was trying to teach her class good manners. She asked, "Michael, if you were on a date having dinner with a nice young lady, how would you tell her that you have to go to the toilet?"

Michael said, "You wait here, I have to go piss."

The teacher screeched, "No no no! That is extremely rude! What about you Peter, how would you say it?"

Peter said, "I am sorry, but I really need to go to the lav. I'll be right back."

"That's better, but it's still not very nice to say the word lav at the dinner table. Right, little Johnny, can you please show us your good manners?"

I would say, "Darling, may I please be excused for a moment? I have to shake hands with a very dear friend of mine, whom I hope you'll get to meet after dinner."

# Mesmerising

A hypnotist asked a dozen audience members to join him on stage. Once they were sitting down, he put them in a trance and said, "Now you are in my power, you will all obey my every command."

The hypnotist gave his first command, "Applaud," and each of the twelve began clapping. "Stop," he ordered, and the twelve stopped.

"Laugh," came the next command, so the twelve started to giggle until he commanded "Stop" once more.

The hypnotist turned to address the rest of the audience, but lost his balance, fell and cried out, "Shit!"

It took a week to get the smell out of the stage.

# The Great Outdoors

A man was camping with his family one weekend. His son said to him, "Dad, Dad, I really need to have a poo!"

Dad replied, "No problem my lad. That's one of the great things about camping. You can poo anywhere you want and not get into trouble."

Ten minutes later Dad saw his son again. "Where did you go?" he asked.

The boy replied, "In your car."

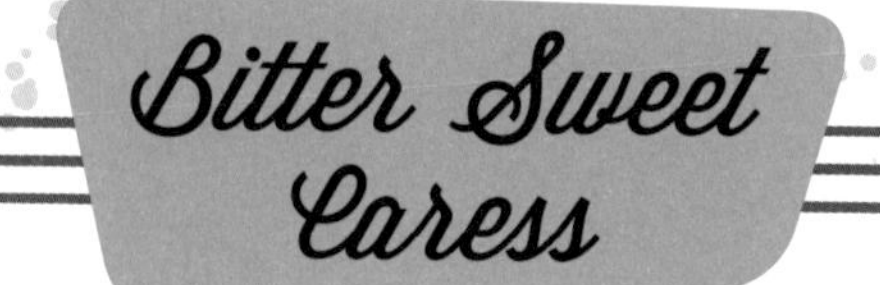

# Bitter Sweet Caress

A rather attractive woman walks up to the bar in a quiet rural pub. She gestures alluringly to the barman who comes over immediately. When he arrives, she seductively signals that he should bring his face close to hers. When he does so, she begins to gently caress his beard which is full and bushy. "Are you the manager?" she asks, softly stroking his face with both hands.

"Actually, no," he replies.

"Can you get him for me? I need to speak to him," she asks, running her hands up beyond his beard and into his hair.

"I'm afraid I can't," breathes the barman – clearly aroused. "Is there anything I can do?"

"Yes there is. I need you to give him a message," she continues huskily, popping a couple of fingers into his mouth and allowing him to suck them gently. "Tell him," she says, "there is no toilet paper in the Ladies."

A MAN WHO WAS ON THE RUN DECIDED TO HIDE IN THE TOILET. POLICE SOON FLUSHED HIM OUT.

## WHAT DO YOU DO IF A BIRD CRAPS ON YOUR CAR?

## DON'T ASK HER FOR A SECOND DATE.

# Limericks

****

### SOME BALLADS OF BREAKING WIND

There once was a young man from Sparta
Who was widely renowned as a farter
On the strength of one bean
He'd fart God Save the Queen
and Beethoven's Moonlight Sonata

While once with the Duchess at tea
She asked, "Do you burp when you pee?"
I said - with some wit -
"Do you fart when you shit?"
And felt it was one up to me

There once was a man from North Ealing
Whose wife found his farts unappealing
As the stench took a hold
She lay in bed, cold
As the duvet came down from the ceiling

# ON THE JOB

A smartphone is a great way to pass the time on the loo, especially if you want to skive from work for an extra few minutes. Careful though, things could go badly wrong.

Here are some tips to ensure a safe iPoo.

## 1. DON'T BE TEMPTED TO ANSWER A CALL

- someone in the next cubicle might flush. Or fart. Or worse.

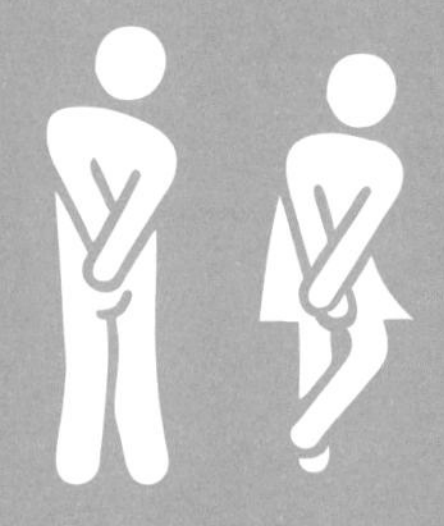

## 2. TURN OFF SOUNDS BEFORE YOU GET THERE

- the Angry Birds music is a dead giveaway.

## 3. IF FLICKING THROUGH YOUR APPS, BE CAREFUL NOT TO TURN ON THE CAMERA

- this could lead to internet stardom or a law-suit. Or both.

## 4. A TOILET PAPER APP WILL NEVER BE AS USEFUL AS IT SOUNDS

- your phone insurance is unlikely to cover that.

## 5. IF YOU PLAY A GAME, DON'T CHEER IF YOU WIN

- think how that sounds in the next cubicle.

## 6. IF SOMEONE TEXTS YOU A JOKE, DON'T LAUGH OUT LOUD

- see number 5...

## 7. DON'T SHARE WHAT YOU'RE DOING RIGHT THAT MINUTE ON FACEBOOK OR TWITTER

- would you want that on your wall??

## 8. DON'T PUT YOUR PHONE IN YOUR SHIRT POCKET WHEN YOU'RE DONE

- think ahead - what will happen when you lean forward to flush?

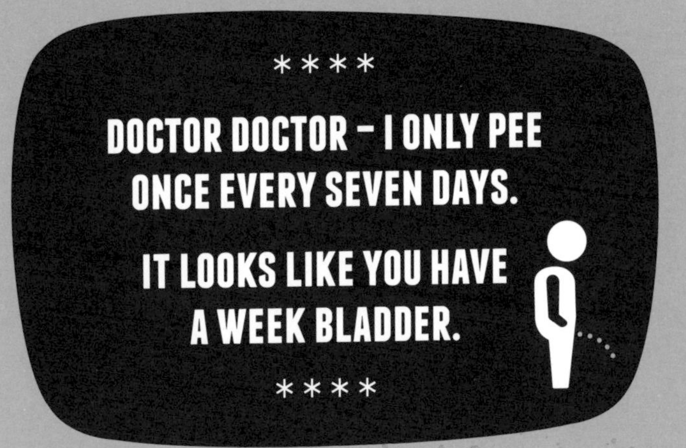

**** ****

"I have found out that there ain't no surer way to find out whether you like people or hate them than to travel with them."

Getting from A to B is often not as straightforward as you might think. We hope you have a smoother passage than some of these.

## Lost In Translation

* * * *

An Inuk was driving through Wales when his car spluttered to a halt. He called the breakdown service and, half an hour later, a local mechanic was giving his car the once over.

After a few moments under the bonnet, the mechanic said, "Hmm, I think you've blown a seal."

"Cheeky sod!" the Inuk fumed. "I think you shag sheep!"

## Directionless

* * * * * * * *

A businessman was checking out of a hotel and asked the receptionist, "Excuse me, but which is the quickest way to Manchester?"

"Are you walking or driving?" she enquired.

"Driving," he said.

"Well, yes, that's definitely the quickest way."

**A MAN WALKED INTO A PUB WITH A LUMP OF TARMAC UNDER HIS ARM. "I'LL HAVE A PINT," HE SAID TO THE BARMAN, "AND ONE FOR THE ROAD."**

## U-turn If You Want To

A man is driving the wrong way up the M1 when police finally catch up and stop him. "Do you know where you're going?" asks the policeman.

"Yes," the man replies, "but it must be rubbish because everyone else is going the other way."

## Getting Warmer

Two guys are hurtling through the mountains on a motorbike when the pillion passenger can't take the cold around his neck any more. They stop for a moment so he can take his jacket off and put it on again, back to front to shield his neck.

Back on the road again, they pass through a couple of small villages when the driver realises he has lost his passenger.

He turns around and speeds back the way he came. In the first village he finds he sees a parked ambulance and a small crowd gathering. He parks the bike and pushes his way into the circle.

He sees two paramedics leaning over his friend and hears, "OK, on the count of three, we'll turn his head round the right way. One… Two…"

# GOOD NEWS

Helen phoned her husband at work. "Ron, I've got good news and bad news about the car."

"Uh oh," said Ron nervously, "give me the good news first."

"The good news," said Helen, "is that the air bag works."

# FUN RUN

**** ****

A salesman has been driving all night and desperately needs some sleep. He stops his car near a popular park and soon nods off. Only a few moments later a jogger knocks on the window and asks, "Excuse me, do you know the time?"

The salesman slurs "7:30" in reply. The jogger thanks him and leaves him to sleep once more. He only catches a few more winks when another jogger knocks on the window.

"Excuse me, do you know the time?" enquires the jogger.

"7:32," snaps the now angry salesman. As the second jogger leaves, the salesman takes out a pen and paper. He writes "I DO NOT KNOW THE TIME!!" on the paper and leaves it visible on his windscreen.

It's not long before he gets to sleep, but once again there is a knock on the window. This jogger gives the man the thumbs up and says, "It's 7:35."

# On Track

Two friends, Barry and John, were on a train from London to Newcastle when an Australian joined them at their table. Barry asked the Aussie, "So, why are you heading to Newcastle?"

He replied, "I've just flown in from Oz, I'm here to see my girlfriend."

Barry was a bit deaf, so he asked John, "What did he say?"

John replied loudly, "He has just flown here from Australia. Going to see his girlfriend."

"Blimey," said Barry, "she must be lovely if you are travelling all this way."

"Yeah, she's great," said the Aussie.

"You what?" said Barry.

"She's great," John echoed.

Barry continued his questioning. "What's so great about her then? Is it the sex?"

The Aussie replied, "Oh yes. She enjoys dressing up in leather and stilettos, being whipped and doing who knows what with a cucumber."

"What?" said Barry.

Exasperated, John said, "He knows your mother."

**WHAT DO YOU DO WHEN YOU SEE A SPACEMAN?**

**PARK YOUR CAR, MAN.**

# Under The Bonnet

A man pushes his car into a garage and asks the mechanic to take a look at why it won't start. He takes a seat in the waiting area and after a few minutes the mechanic appears and says, "All done."

"That was quick," says the man. "What's the story with it?"

"Just crap in the carburettor," replies the mechanic.

"Oh," says the man, "how often do I have to do that?"

## **** BUM STEER ****

A man is looking under his bonnet at the side of the road. A tramp walks by and asks, "Trouble?"

"Yeah," says the man, "piston broke."

"Ah," replies the tramp, "me too, mate, me too."

**I SAW AN AA MAN AT THE WHEEL OF HIS VAN CRYING HIS EYES OUT. I THINK HE WAS HEADING FOR A BREAKDOWN.**

## Off The Rails

A train is crawling along the track and eventually comes to a complete halt. The passengers begin mumbling and after a few minutes the driver is seen out the window, walking by the train. A rather annoyed lady shouts to him, "What the hell is going on?"

The driver replies, "There's a cow on the track."

Ten minutes pass and the train moves on, but still very slowly. It's only minutes before it stops once more and the driver is soon spotted outside. The same lady shouts out, "What happened, did we catch up with the cow again?"

## Pensioner's Passage

A husband and wife of advanced years were on a train taking them on holiday for the first time in years. "Oh god, Arthur," exclaimed the wife, "I left the oven on!"

"Don't worry Doreen," he replied, "the house won't burn down, I left the bath running."

## Mile Sigh Club

A man is on a plane sitting in the window seat when, an hour into the flight, he gets up to have a pee. When he gets back he finds someone sitting in his seat.

Angered, he asks, "What the hell do you think you're doing in my seat?"

The stranger replies, "Sorry, I thought you'd got off."

## Brace Yourself

A captain is struggling to remain in control of his plane so he announces that everyone should get ready for an emergency landing.

The cabin crew get straight to work ensuring that everyone is prepared.

The head stewardess goes into the cockpit to check with the captain. The captain asks, "Are all the passengers ready?"

"Almost," says the stewardess. "Everyone is in their seat and in the brace position, except for a lawyer who is still handing out business cards."

# Head In The Clouds

About an hour into a transatlantic flight, the captain announced, "Ladies and gentlemen, one of our engines has failed but there is nothing to be concerned about. We still have three engines left. However, our flight will now take about one hour longer than scheduled. We apologise for the inconvenience."

Twenty minutes later the captain announced, "I regret to report that one more of our engines has failed. There is still nothing to worry about as we have two engines left. However our arrival will now be delayed by about two hours."

It was another fifteen minutes later when the captain announced, "This is quite unusual, but unfortunately one more engine has failed. Not to worry, however. Believe it or not we are still able to fly successfully with just one engine. However our delay will now be at least three hours."

In the cabin, one passenger turned to another and said, "Oh dear, if we lose one more engine, we'll be up here all day."

* * * *

**PATIENCE:** A QUALITY YOU ADMIRE IN THE DRIVER BEHIND YOU AND DETEST IN THE DRIVER AHEAD OF YOU.

A JUMPER CABLE WALKS INTO A BAR. THE BARMAN SAYS, "I HOPE YOU'RE NOT THINKING ABOUT STARTING SOMETHING."

Plop-O-Matic

## Limericks

### SOME VERSES ABOUT VOYAGE

I'd been running with all of my might
When the check-in desk came into sight
I had made it there
With seconds to spare
To find out they'd cancelled my flight

I enjoy taking time at the keel
And getting a price that's a steal
So I hired a row boat
When I got a cheap quote
And found it was quite an oar deal

Both I and the bike that I'd hired
Took a break before we expired
Before going to town
We had to lie down
As both I and the bike were two-tyred

# SUTURE SELF

"Isn't it a bit unnerving that doctors call what they do 'practice'?"

*George Carlin*

Some say laughter is the best medicine, but I'm sure my chemist would disagree with that. Either way, stick your tongue out, cough and enjoy some moments of medical mirth.

# All Fingers And Thumbs

Pete was setting up his brand new rotary saw when he slipped and managed to cut all of his fingers off. He screamed out in pain and ran to the local hospital as fast as he could. A nurse came to assess him and said, "Sorry, but without your fingers, we can only stop the bleeding. Go back and get them and we'll try to sew them back on."

"OK," said an already tired Pete, who turned and ran out of the hospital. He returned an hour later and found the same nurse. She said, "Great, you're back. Do you have your fingers?"

"No", replied Pete, "I couldn't pick them up."

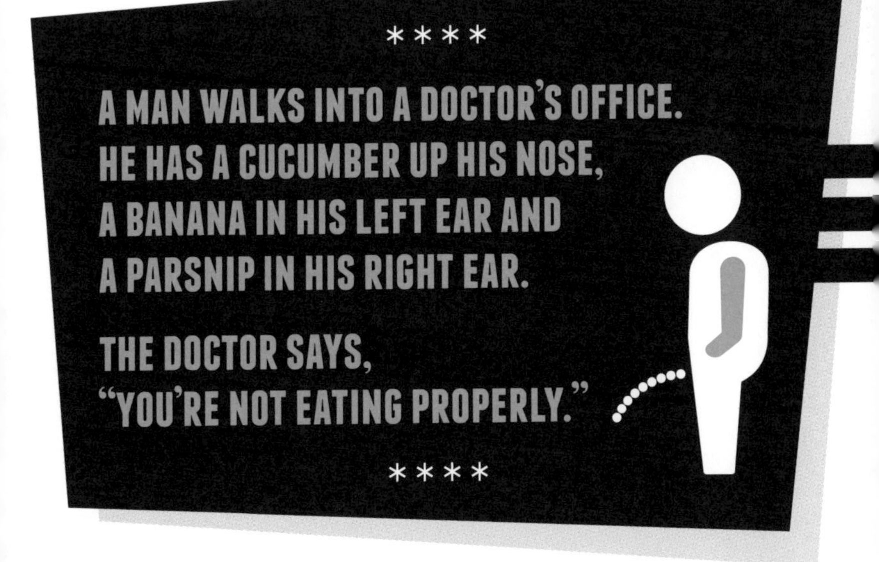

## Stress Balls

A husband and wife go to the doctor's for a check-up.

Afterwards, the doctor calls the wife in alone, and says, "Your husband is suffering from severe stress. If you don't do as I say he will die. Each morning, give him oral sex. Cook him a meal every night, and be pleasant at all times. Don't nag him, and give him sex at least three times a week. In a few years, he will be fully fit again."

On the way home, the husband turns to his wife and asks, "So what did the doctor say then?"

The wife replies, "You're going to die."

## Wrist Action Reaction

**After weeks worrying about his eyesight, John finally goes to see an optician who tells him he must stop masturbating immediately.**

**"Why," says John, "is it making me go blind?"**

**"No," replies the optician, "but it is upsetting everyone in the waiting room."**

# He's A Ten

**** ****

Jeff sat in the doctor's office awaiting the results of weeks of tests. He asked the doctor, "Come on Doc, tell me straight. How long have I got?"

The doctor said, "Ten."

Jeff begged, "Ten what? Ten years? Ten months? Ten weeks?"

The doctor shook his head. "Nine…"

# It's Purely Medicinal

As the doctor completed an examination of the patient, he said, "I can't find a cause for your complaint. Frankly, I think it's due to drinking."

"In that case," slurred the patient, "I'll come back when you're sober."

**"DOCTOR, I'VE BADLY BRUISED MY PENIS IN A SURFING ACCIDENT."**

**"DID YOU FALL OFF YOUR BOARD?"**

**"NO, I HAD TO SLAM MY LAPTOP SHUT RATHER QUICKLY."**

## GEORGE HAS 50 BARS OF CHOCOLATE IN HIS DRAWER. HE EATS 37 OF THEM. WHAT DOES HE HAVE NOW?

## DIABETES.

# *Corpsing*

First year students at Medical School were receiving their first anatomy class with a real dead human body. They all gathered around the surgery table with the body covered by a white sheet.

The professor started the class by telling them, "To be a doctor requires two important qualities. The first is that you should not be disgusted by anything involving the human body."

As an example, the professor pulled back the sheet, stuck his finger in the arse of the corpse, withdrew it and stuck his finger in his mouth.

"Now it's your turn," he told his students. The students freaked out, hesitated for several minutes, but eventually took turns sticking a finger in the arse of the dead body and sucking on it.

When everyone had finished, the professor looked at them and told them, "The second most important quality is observation. I stuck in my middle finger and sucked on my index finger."

# Specimental

A doctor wanted to do a sperm count of his 85-year-old patient as part of his physical exam. The doctor gave the man a jar and said, "Take this jar home and bring back a semen sample tomorrow."

The next day the 85-year-old man reappeared at the doctor's office and gave him the jar, which was completely empty.

The doctor asked what had happened and the man explained, "Well, doc, it's like this. First I tried with my right hand, but nothing. Then I tried with my left hand, but still nothing.

"Then I asked my wife for help. She tried with her right hand, then with her left, still nothing. She tried with her mouth, first with her teeth in, then with her teeth out, still nothing.

"We even called up Miriam, the lady next door, and she tried too, first with both hands, then an armpit, and she even tried squeezing it between her knees, but still nothing."

The doctor was shocked. "You asked your neighbour?"

The old man replied, "Yep, none of us could get the jar open."

## Sunbathing Blues

A guy fell asleep on the beach for several hours and got horrible sunburn. He went to the hospital and was promptly admitted after being diagnosed with second-degree burns. He was already starting to blister and was in agony.

The attending doctor prescribed a suitable IV drip, a sedative and a Viagra pill every four hours.

The nurse, rather astounded, said, "What good will Viagra do him?"

The doctor replied, "It'll keep the bed sheets off his legs."

**AFTER SWALLOWING SOME MONEY, A MAN ASKED THE X-RAY TECHNICIAN, "DO YOU SEE ANY CHANGE IN ME?"**

A man charges through the doors of the A&E department in an Essex hospital, absolutely covered in blood. A doctor runs up to him and asks, "Where are you bleeding from?"

"Colchester," the man replies.

## Three Samples

A 90-year-old man goes to the doctor for his yearly physical with his wife tagging along.

When the doctor enters the examination room he tells the old man, "I need a urine sample, a stool sample, and a sperm sample."

The old man, being hard of hearing, looks at his wife and yells, "WHAT? What did he say? What's he want?"

His wife yells back, "He needs your underwear."

## **** HIPPOCRATIC ODES ****

There once was a young man called Ben
Who went out to pull nurses again
He met one called Kate
Had her laughing by eight
But she had him in stitches by ten

A nurse who was getting quite bored
Grabbed a doctor and mounted his sword
The passion soon passed
And she transferred at last
Now she's on the maternity ward

# Doctor DOCTOR...

... I keep thinking I'm a cashpoint.
Don't worry, you're just suffering from withdrawal.

... I've got a lettuce leaf sticking out of my bottom.
That's just the tip of the iceberg.

... I think I'm a pack of cards.
I'm busy now, come back later and I'll deal with you then.

... Are you sure this cream will clear up my spots?
I never make rash promises.

... I keep thinking I'm a nun.
You have a Mother Superiority complex.

... I've nearly become invisible.
I can see you're not all there.

... I've broken my neck.
Keep your chin up.

... I keep hallucinating about Mickey Mouse and Donald Duck.
How long have you been having these Disney spells?

... I keep thinking I'm shrinking.
Wait here a moment, I'm afraid you'll have to be a little patient.

... I keep seeing an insect spinning round my head.
It's just the bug that's going round.

... I keep thinking I'm an airport.
I'm sorry, it's terminal.

## Who Wants To Live Forever?

A man went to see the doctor. "Doc, do you think I can live for another fifty years?"

Doctor: "Do you drink?"

Man: "No!"

Doctor: "Do you smoke?"

Man: "No!"

Doctor: "Do you have kinky sex, gamble or drive fast cars?"

Man: "Certainly not!"

Doctor: "Then why do you want to live another fifty years?"

## Bedside Manners

A doctor and his wife were arguing about their sex life. "You just don't pay any attention to my needs," she said.

The doctor replied, "I do. It's you. You are dreadful in bed." And he stormed off to work.

Mid-morning, the doctor realised he had overreacted and decided to call his wife at home. The phone rang and rang before she answered. When she did, the doctor asked, "Why did it take you so long to answer the phone?"

She replied, "I was getting a second opinion."

## Face Off

A rather vain man went into hospital to have some plastic surgery. He wanted a facelift to smooth out his wrinkles.

After the operation he woke up to find there had been a mistake. Rather than a facelift he had been given breast implants.

"What the hell is going on?" he screamed at the doctor.

"We're very sorry," the doctor replied, "but at least no one is looking at your wrinkles any more."

# RIGHT ON QUEUE

* * * *

A tired nurse walks into a post office, totally exhausted after an 18-hour shift.

When she gets to the front of the queue, she pulls a rectal thermometer out of her purse and tries to write with it. When she realises her mistake, she looks at the confused assistant and says, "Brilliant. Bloody brilliant. Some arsehole's got my pen."

Pull FOR Flush

# Brotherly Love

A pregnant woman has a car accident and goes into a coma. After six months out cold, she wakes up to find that she is no longer pregnant. Frantically, she asks the doctor what happened.

The doctor replies, "You had twins – a boy and a girl. There's nothing to worry about, they are fine. Your brother has been looking after them, he had them christened..."

"What?" exclaims the woman, cutting the doctor short. "Not that idiot. What has he called them?"

"Well, he called the girl Denise," says the doctor.

"Oh," says the new mother, "that's a nice name. I like Denise. What's the boy's name?"

The doctor replies, "Denephew."

* * * *

Have you genned up on the John? Do you know the facts of the facilities? Check out your knowledge of loo lore with this quiz!

### 1. THE JAPANESE LOVE THEIR TECHIE TOILETS – WHICH OF THESE IS REAL?

a. A toilet that can save penalty kicks of up to 160km/h
b. A half toilet/half motorcycle that runs on human biogas
c. A toilet that can be controlled by a smartphone

## 2. WHO INVENTED THE FLUSH TOILET?

a. Thomas Crapper of Thomas Crapper and Sons
b. Sir John Harrington, godson of Queen Elizabeth I
c. Lord Alfred Cistern, an 18th-century member of the Privy Council

## 3. WHAT DID RICH TUDOR FOLK USE TO WIPE THEIR BEHINDS?

a. Dyed wool
b. Swan feathers
c. The poor

## 4. WHICH OF THESE WAS NOT A STYLE OF LOO SOLD BY THOMAS CRAPPER?

a. Deluge
b. Niagara
c. Tornado
d. Dump-matic 5000

## 5. WHICH OF THESE PHRASES DOES NOT ORIGINATE FROM THE LOO?

a. On a roll
b. Wrong end of the stick
c. The penny dropped

## 6. WHICH OF THESE DID OFFICIALS DO TO PREPARE FOR THE CORONATION OF QUEEN ELIZABETH II AT WESTMINSTER ABBEY?

a. Install a heated loo just for the Queen's use
b. Test how loud the flush of every toilet was
c. Ban anyone below an Earl from using a toilet

How did you do? Turn the page for the answers.

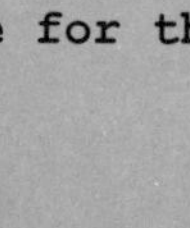

# Answers

**** ****

1. All are real! Loo manufacturer Toto built the goalkeeping and motorcycle loos as publicity stunts. Lixil began selling smartphone-controlled loos in 2013. Be careful texting on the loo.

2. b. Sir John Harrington built two flushing toilets, one for himself and one for his godmother, Queen Elizabeth I, in 1594. It's a myth that Thomas Crapper invented it, but he knew a good thing when he flushed it.

3. a. Dyed wool. Though a few may have employed the poor...

4. d. Dump-matic 5000. If you didn't get that one right, give up now.

5. a. On a roll. "The penny dropped" relates to dropping a penny in the slot to use a Victorian public loo, just like "spend a penny". Romans using a public loo used a stick with a wad of damp cloth to wipe their behinds. You really did not want to get hold of the "wrong end of the stick".

6. b. They got sound technicians from the BBC to help check if any amount of toilet flushing would disturb the ceremony or at worst be recorded for posterity. Thankfully, it was not possible for events to be disturbed by a Royal Flush.

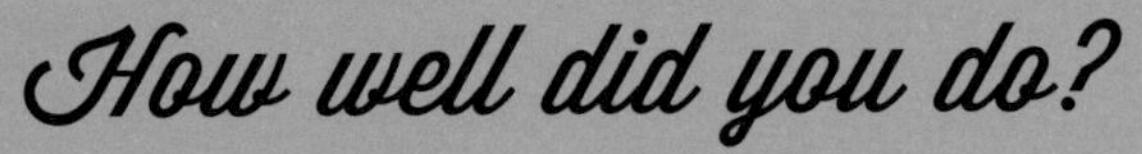


* * *

**0 TO 2 – DOWN THE DRAIN**

**3 TO 5 – FLUSHED WITH PRIDE**

**6 – ON THE THRONE!**

* * *

# Service WITH A Snarl

"So I went down my local
ice-cream shop, and said
'I want to buy an ice-cream.'

He said, 'Hundreds and
thousands?'

I said, 'We'll start
with one.'"

*Tommy Cooper*

They call it Customer Service. Whether you seek help from an assistant, another shopper or the support team, as a customer you often feel you have been well and truly serviced.

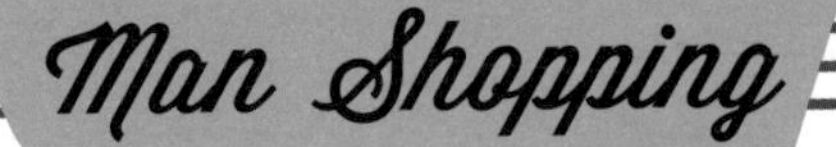

# Man Shopping

A wife asked her husband, "Joe, can you pop out and buy a pint of milk, and if they have eggs, get six."

The husband went to the corner shop and came back a few minutes later with six pints of milk. His wife asked, "Why on earth did you get six?"

He replied, "They had eggs."

# Chemist Conundrum

****

Lloyd goes into a chemist to buy some condoms. Unfortunately, he has a really sore throat and can't ask the man behind the counter for his favourite brand. After much croaking and pointing, Lloyd is about to give up – then he has an idea.

He undoes his trousers, takes out his penis and lays it on the counter with a £5 note. The chemist says, "OK then," does exactly the same, then pockets both fivers and zips himself up again.

Lloyd, clearly angry, shakes his head and waves his hands. The chemist says, "It's your fault – if you're not prepared to lose, you shouldn't gamble."

## Fit The Best

A salesman telephoned his customer. "Mrs Smith, our company installed double glazing throughout your house over a year ago, and you still haven't sent us a single penny."

"Excuse me," replied Mrs Smith, "but you promised me the windows would pay for themselves in 12 months."

## Revealing Situation

A young woman was in a clothes shop trying on a very low-cut dress. She asked the sales assistant if it was too low-cut.

"Do you have hair on your chest?" the assistant asked.

"No," said the woman.

"Then, yes, it's too low-cut."

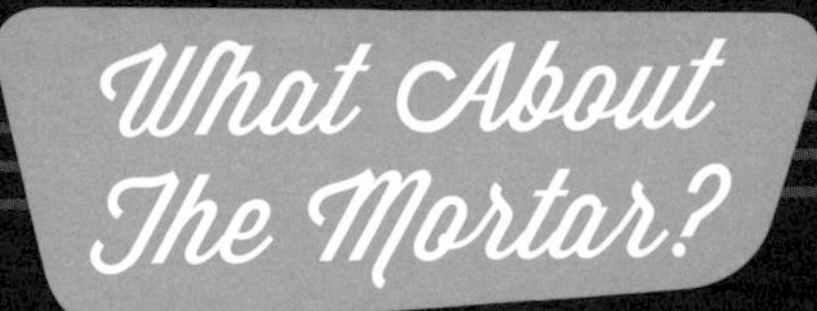


A man goes into his local DIY shop and asks for 15,000 bricks.

"Can I ask what they are for?" asks the man behind the counter.

"I'm building a barbecue."

"Wow, that's a lot of bricks for one barbecue."

"Not really, I live on the 12th floor."

## Signs Of The Times

A shopkeeper had been running his business successfully for some years when a competitor moved into the shop on the left. As soon as the shop opened, a big sign went up above the door reading "Lowest Prices".

The shopkeeper soon had more troubles when another competitor opened on his right side, with a bigger sign above their door that read "Greatest Deals".

So the shopkeeper had a sign made for his own shop. In even bigger letters, it read "Main Entrance".

**I SET UP A SHOP THAT SELLS "CLOSED" SIGNS. I HAVEN'T HAD A SINGLE CUSTOMER.**

# What's In A NAME?

Crap 'O' Matic

When you combine A Nation of Shopkeepers with the British Sense of Humour, you are bound to get some outrageous results. We thank the following shopkeepers for giving us a smile on the high street.

## SERVICES

Turnham Green, dry cleaner: Turn 'em Clean
Oxfordshire, plumber: The Lone Drainer – he come pronto
Merseyside, driving school: L Passo
London, gardeners: Tree Wise Men
London, dog spa: Pugs and Kisses
Chatham, pet nanny service: Hairy Poppins
Notting Hill, picture framers: Frame Set and Match
Dartford, paper recycling: Pulp Friction
West Midlands, nails and tanning: Beauty and the Beach
Dorchester, beauty salon: Facial Attraction

## SPECIALIST RETAILERS

Croydon, second-hand records: The Vinyl Frontier
Penge, teddy bear shop: Bearly Trading
Liverpool, fridges: Sellfridges

Teddington, furniture: Sofa So Good
Leeds, printer supplies: Alan Cartridge
Ashford, glaziers: Pane in the Glass
Wimbledon, fireplaces: Grate Expectations

## FOOD

South Wales, fish & chips: A Fish called Rhondda
Sheffield, fish & chips: A Salt N Battered
Walkley, fish & chips: Codrophenia
Battersea, fish & chips: Battersea Cods Home
Slough, fish & chips: The Prawnbrokers
Ayr, Indian restaurant: Ayr India
Radford, Indian restaurant: Balti Towers
Crouch End, Thai restaurant: ThaiTanic
Dartmoor, mobile snack bar: The Hound of the Basket Meals
Cornwall, mobile snack bar: The Star Chip Enterprise
Argyll, health food shop: Oban Sesame
Rugby, fast food: Pizza The Action
Torquay, sandwich bar: Licence to Fill

## HAIRDRESSERS/BARBERS

Bedfordshire: Lunatic Fringe
South Yorkshire: Director's Cut
Brighton: Barber Blacksheep
Buckinghamshire: Curls Aloud
Bristol: Curl Up and Dye

## AND LET'S NOT FORGET:

Blood, Sweat and Shears, Clip Joint, Debon Hair, Hair Razor, The Locks Smith, The Hairtaker, Get Your Locks Off

# ALL THE PATTER

****

A sales assistant asked the manager how to handle people who complained about the current prices compared to the low prices in the good old days.

"Just act surprised and tell them you didn't think that they looked old enough to remember them."

## Next Customer Please

A man was in the supermarket checkout queue with a mountain of shopping in his trolley.

A little old lady joined the queue behind him. She had just a pint of milk and a loaf of bread in her basket. The man turned to her and said, "Aah, is that all you've got?"

She gave a calm smile and replied, "Yes, dear."

"Well," he said, "you'd best piss off - this lot's gonna take ages."

****

DEAR CUSTOMER SERVICES, FIRST OF ALL, YOU SHOULD KNOW I AM TYPING THIS WITH MY MIDDLE FINGER...

I WAS IN A SUPERMARKET CAR PARK WHEN I SAW THIS BLOKE TRYING TO GET A TROLLEY INTO HIS CAR BOOT. "YOU CAN'T DO THAT," I SAID RATHER POINTEDLY.

"I BLOODY CAN," HE RETORTED, "I JUST PAID A QUID FOR IT."

## Bargaining Skills

Sarah was in the market looking for bargains. She went up to a stallholder and asked, "How much are these mangoes?"

"£1 for two," came the reply.

"How much for just one?" Sarah probed.

"75p."

"In that case," said Sarah, "I'll have the other one."

# WARNING
## May Insult Intelligence

Going shopping can be a painful process, but it gets even worse when your purchases rub salt into your retail wounds. All these are genuine messages from various products, but it's hard to tell whether they are meant to help, insult or just plain confuse us.

- On a bag of crisps: "You could be a winner! No purchase necessary. Details inside."
- On a bar of soap: "Directions: Use like regular soap."
- On a tiramisu dessert (printed on bottom of box): "Do not turn upside down."
- On a birthday card for a 1-year-old: "Not suitable for children aged 36 months or less."
- On a pushchair: "Caution: Remove infant before folding for storage."
- On the barrel of a .22 calibre rifle: "Warning: Misuse may cause injury or death."
- On children's cough medicine: "Do not drive a car or operate machinery after taking this medication."
- On Christmas lights: "For indoor or outdoor use only."

- On a Japanese food processor: "Not to be used for the other use."
- On a dessert box: "Product will be hot after heating."
- On an airline packet of nuts: "Instructions: Open packet, eat nuts."
- On a child's Superman costume: "Wearing of this garment does not enable you to fly."
- On a chain saw: "Do not attempt to stop chain with your hand."
- On a curling iron: "For external use only."
- On bicycle shin pads: "Shin pads cannot protect any part of the body they do not cover."
- On a can of self-defence pepper spray: "May irritate eyes."
- On a toilet bowl cleaning brush: "Do not use orally."

...and if you need this warning, please never go shopping again:

- On a packet of peanuts: "Contains nuts."

****

A CHEESEBURGER SAID TO THE BARMAN, "PINT OF LAGER PLEASE."

THE BARMAN SAID, "SORRY, WE DON'T SERVE FOOD."

****

## Udder Disaster

A farm-hand had just connected the cows up to the brand new milking machine when he thought he might test the machine on himself. So he dropped his trousers, took out his little friend and placed it inside the "udder sucker". He turned the machine on and, after a few minutes of pleasure, had a great orgasm.

The farm-hand looked at the control panel, but could not find any off switch. He tried various dials and switches, but the collector was stuck fast and kept on sucking. He watched his member going purple and he was just about to pass out when he remembered he had his mobile with him. He called customer services and explained, "I've got your new machine, it won't come off the udders and I can't shut it down."

"Don't worry sir," said the voice at the end of the line, "it will turn itself off automatically after it has collected two gallons."

## Good Reception

A woman runs into hotel reception and says to the clerk, "I'm in quite a hurry, can you check me out?"

He looks her up and down, and then says, "Not bad. Not bad at all."

# Re-tail-wind

A lady walks into a high-class jewellery shop. She browses around and spots a beautiful diamond bracelet and walks over to inspect it. As she bends over to look more closely, she inadvertently lets out a tiny fart.

Embarrassed, she looks around nervously to see if anyone has noticed her little accident when she sees the salesman standing right behind her.

Acting professionally, the salesman greets the lady with, "Good day, Madam. How may I help you today?"

Awkwardly, she asks, "Sir, what is the price of this lovely bracelet?"

He answers, "Madam, if you farted just looking at it, you are going to shit yourself when I tell you the price."

**CINDY WALKED INTO A PET SHOP AND ASKED, "DO YOU HAVE ANY KITTENS GOING CHEAP?"**

**"NO," REPLIED THE OWNER, "THEY ALL GO MEOW."**

VACANT

ACME

# LOVE **** And **** CARNAGE

"A successful man is one who makes more money than his wife can spend. A successful woman is one who can find such a man."

The battle of the sexes rages on. Men and women may understand one another in the future. Until then, sit back and enjoy the skirmishes as best you can.

## Tally Ho

"Come on Dave," said Michelle, "we've got no other secrets. It's time you told me how many women you've slept with."

"No," replied Dave, "you won't like it."

Michelle insisted. "We've been married for years now, what difference could it make?"

"Well, if you're sure," said Dave reluctantly. "Let's see, one… two… three… you… five… six…"

## Rule Of Three

The three stages of sex after marriage:

- Tri-weekly
- Try weekly
- Try weakly

**THERE ONCE WAS A MAN NAME OF MORT**
**WHO PUBLICLY CHOSE TO CAVORT**
**HE SHAGGED HIS WIFE TINA**
**AT WEMBLEY ARENA**
**AND THREE TIMES A WEEK AT EARL'S COURT**

## Mourning After

Judy wakes up in an unfamiliar bed. She rolls over and, on seeing the guy next to her, starts to remember a wild night of drink and sex. Then as she looks around, Judy sees the walls are lined with shelves full of teddy bears – from baby ones on the floor to daddy ones near the ceiling.

She is hesitant to mention the bears, so when the guy wakes up, she says, "Wow, what a night! How was it for you?"

"Well," he says glumly, "you can have any prize from the bottom shelf."

## Good Morning, Good Morning

**A weary wife is in the kitchen one morning when she hears a key scraping at the front door. Eventually it slots into place, turns and the door opens. In staggers her husband who comes into the kitchen and slumps at the table.**

**"You've been out all damned night!" says the wife. "You'd better have a good reason for strolling back here at 7:30 in the morning."**

**"Yep," he replies. "Breakfast."**

# Swings And Roundabouts

Beth was telling her friend Sophie about her home life. "My husband was unhappy with what he called 'my mood swings'. He bought me a mood ring the other day so he would be able to monitor my moods."

"What does it do?" asked Sophie.

"Well," said Beth, "we've discovered that when I'm in a good mood, it turns green. When I'm in a bad mood, it leaves a ****ing great big red mark on his forehead."

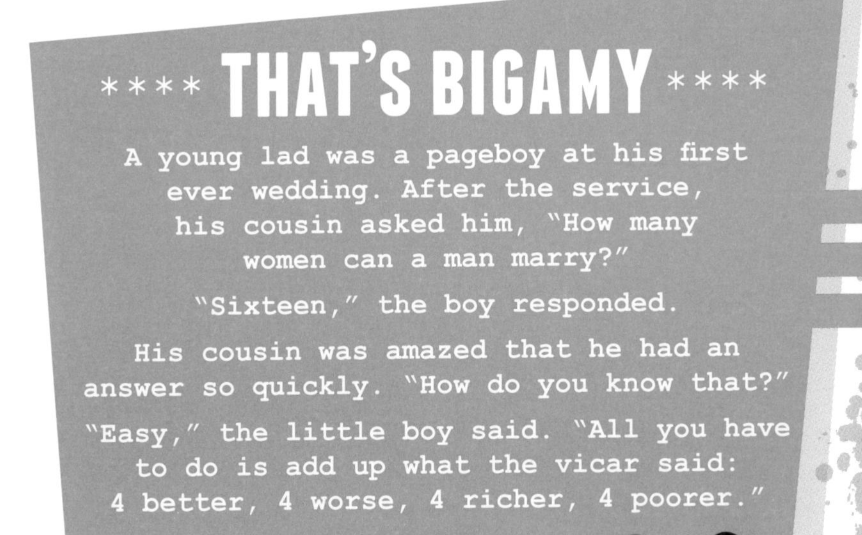

## **** THAT'S BIGAMY ****

A young lad was a pageboy at his first ever wedding. After the service, his cousin asked him, "How many women can a man marry?"

"Sixteen," the boy responded.

His cousin was amazed that he had an answer so quickly. "How do you know that?"

"Easy," the little boy said. "All you have to do is add up what the vicar said: 4 better, 4 worse, 4 richer, 4 poorer."

# Dear Diaries

## HER DIARY, OCTOBER 13TH

I'd been out shopping with the girls, and when I got back he was being very quiet. I asked what was wrong and he just mumbled.

I cooked his favourite dinner, but he was still being distant and barely said a word.

We watched a film on the telly, but he was wasn't paying attention. He was staring into space most of the time.

At 11, I said I was going to bed and asked him to come with me. He didn't follow straight away - in fact I was surprised he joined me in bed at all. I kissed him, cuddled him and made love to him, but his heart wasn't in it. He gave me a small, sad smile, then rolled over and went to sleep without saying anything.

I'm sure it's over, he must have found someone else. All I could do was cry myself to sleep.

## HIS DIARY, OCTOBER 13TH

United lost. Bugger. Got a shag though.

**A SUCCESSFUL MARRIAGE IS BASED ON TWO THINGS.**

**NEITHER OF WHICH I KNOW.**

A woman was showing off to her friends. "You see my new ring. This has the Harrison Diamond. It's worth an absolute fortune. Unfortunately though, it comes with a terrible curse."

"Wow," said one of her friends. "What is the curse?"

"Mr Harrison."

## Home Help

A wealthy businessman was on a trip abroad. He called home and a new maid answered. He asked, "Can I speak to my wife?"

"No," said the maid, "she's upstairs in bed with her lover."

"Right", said the man, "get my shotgun, go upstairs and kill them both!"

The phone went quiet for a while, then the businessman heard two loud shots. After a few moments, the maid was back on the line, "What do you want me to do with the bodies?"

"Throw them in the pool!" he exclaimed.

The maid enquired, "What pool?"

Puzzled, the businessman asked, "This is 496 1542 isn't it?"

"Ever since we got married, my wife has tried to change me," Bill poured his heart out to the barman. "She got me to stop drinking, smoking and running around until all hours of the night. She taught me how to dress well, enjoy the fine arts, gourmet cooking, classical music, even how to invest in the stock market. Enough's enough – I'm leaving her."

The barman enquired, "Are you bitter because she changed you so much?"

"I'm not bitter. She just isn't good enough for me."

## Trigger Happy

A blonde came home from work one day and found her husband in bed with another woman. She was so devastated that she grabbed her gun from the bedside table and put it up to her head threatening to commit suicide.

Her husband screamed, "No! No! Please don't do it, I am so sorry!"

The blonde said, "Shut up! You're next!"

## Under Where?

A frustrated wife decided her sex life needed spicing up so she went shopping and picked up a pair of crotchless panties.

She went home and donned the new panties and selected a short skirt to go with them. She greeted her husband when he came home from work and sat across from him sipping a glass of wine.

She slowly spread her legs… "Would you like some of this?"

"No way!" he exclaimed. "Look what it's done to your knickers!"

## Feature Comparison

Gordon asked his wife, "What do like best about me? Is it my rugged, handsome face or my gorgeous, sexy body?"

She looked him up and down for a moment and said, "Your sense of humour."

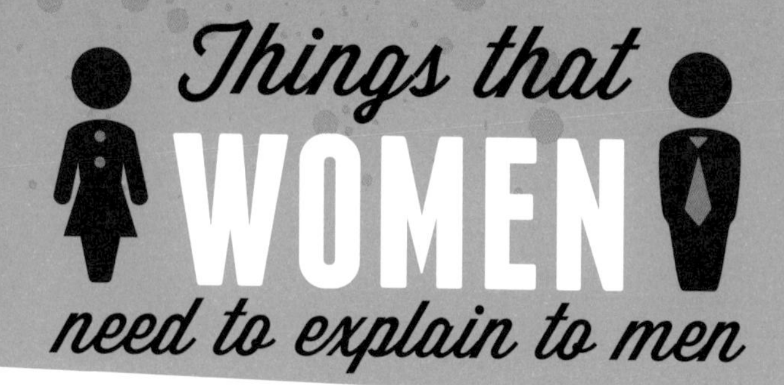


- Why do beds need cushions on them?
- Why are your most expensive shoes the ones you wear the least – and can only sit down in?
- Why can't you go to the toilet without backup?
- Why do you clean the house ready for the cleaners?
- What is the point of pot pourri?
- Do we have a kitchen gadget that you have used more than once?
- Who needs to visit for us ever to use the "best crockery"?
- Why is bra singular and panties plural?
- Why is voting on X-Factor more important than voting in the election?
- Why do you look cute wearing just socks and I look like an idiot?
- What, exactly, do nutri-ceramides and fruit micro-oils do for your hair?
- Who are those short people living in the house?

# Things that MEN need to explain to women

- Why is nosepicking a spectator sport?
- Why does helping with the washing deserve a medal?
- Why can you only cook outdoors?
- How is Formula One in any way interesting?
- Why do you have a full toolbox when you only use a hammer and screwdriver?
- Can you really tell the difference between more than three types of beer?
- When does a toy become an action figure?
- Why can you recall who won the cup in 1993, but not our anniversary?
- Do you really think you look good with a ponytail?
- Is it possible to know someone for more than five minutes without giving them a nickname?
- Why do you think pizza and a belch is foreplay?
- Why is Jeremy Clarkson?

## Joy And Pain

**A husband and wife are lying in bed. He says, "I am going to make you the happiest woman in the world."**

**She says, "I'll miss you."**

## Points Of View

Frank came home from work and found his wife Stella watching MasterChef on the television. He asked, "Why do you bother watching that? You can't cook to save your life."

Stella replied, "So what? You watch porn, don't you?"

## With Compliments

**Tired of a bland sex life, a man asked his wife during a lovemaking session, "How come you never tell me when you have an orgasm?"**

**She glanced at him casually and replied, "You're never home!"**

A woman walked into the kitchen to find her husband darting around with a fly swatter. "What on earth are you doing?" she asked.

"Hunting flies," he responded.

"Oh, killing any?" she asked.

"Yep, three males, two females," he replied.

Intrigued, she asked, "How can you tell?"

He responded, "Three were on a beer can, two were on the phone."

## Touched By Your Presents

My wife was very annoyed that I had forgotten our anniversary. Again. She told me, "You need to make up for this one, Jack. On the driveway tomorrow, there had better be something that goes from 0-60 in the blink of an eye."

So I made a few calls and the next morning she looked out the window to see a new pair of bathroom scales.

## WHY DID THE MEXICAN SHOOT HIS WIFE?

# A LITTLE ROOM To Think

"I never make stupid mistakes.
Only very, very clever ones."

John Peel

Did you hear about the mathematician who had a problem with constipation? He worked it out with a pencil. Here's your chance to work a few things out for yourself - pencil purely optional.

The answers can be found on page 68.

## 1. JOHN IN THE JOHN

John is very particular when it comes to his loo. He wants everything organised, including the toilet paper.

He has 7 rolls of toilet paper, but he wants to lay them in 6 rows of 3 rolls. How does he do it?

## 2. STORAGE SOLUTIONS

It's time to tidy up the toilet. How many rolls of toilet paper can you put, one at a time, onto an empty shelf?

## 3. BRUSH WORK

Can you move two loo brushes to make two triangles?

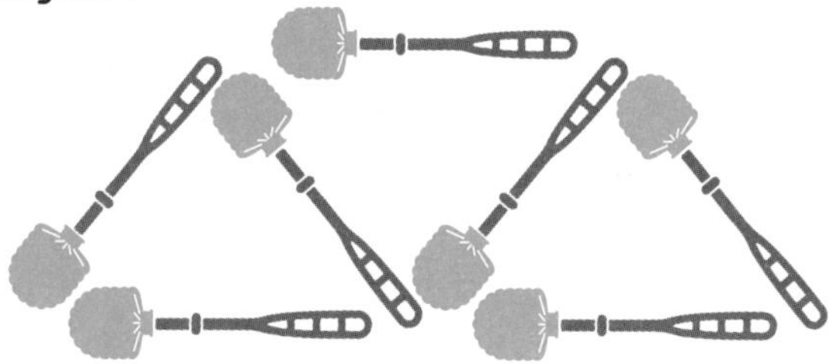

## 4. AGAINST THE CLOCK

Len and Den are hired to clean the office loos. When they work together it takes them 80 minutes to clean them all, both working at top speed.

If Len cleans them all on his own, it takes him 120 minutes.

How long would it take Den to do the job by himself?

## 5. THE CALL OF NATURE

Boar Grills is camping in the woods and has just dug a latrine. It is 1m long, 50cm wide and 35cm deep.

How much earth is in the latrine?

## 6. PO-CD

John is organising his loo rolls again.

This time he is numbering the sheets on a roll. If he numbers the first 100 sheets from 1 to 100, how many times will he write a 7?

## 7. THE RIGHT CHANGE

Joy is at Marylebone train station and desperately needs the loo.

She needs 30p to get through the barrier so she looks in her purse. In there she finds just two coins, both smaller than 50p and one of them is not a 10 pence piece.

Is she going to pay her way or jump the barrier?

## 8. PILLAGE

Jeff needs to take a laxative, but his pills have got mixed up.

He has nine pills but they all look identical and only one of them is a laxative. Jeff knows that his laxative pill is slightly lighter than the others and, luckily, he has a pair of scales.

What is the least number of weighings Jeff can do to be sure of finding the right pill?

## 9. BRUSH UP

Here is your starting position for some more loo brush shenanigans:

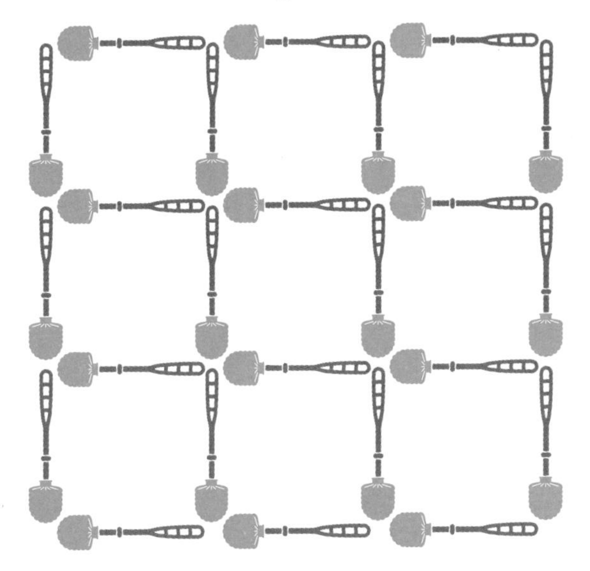

This time, can you:

a. Take 6 loo brushes to leave 5 squares

b. Take 6 loo brushes to leave 3 squares

c. Take 8 loo brushes to leave 3 squares

d. Take 4 loo brushes to leave 5 squares. (There are two ways to do this – try to find both!)

## 10. SPEND A PENNY

Arthur went to the supermarket and bought a new toilet roll holder and a toilet roll.

If the toilet roll holder was £10 more than the toilet roll and the total price was £11, then how much did each item cost?

1. John lays out his toilet rolls like this:

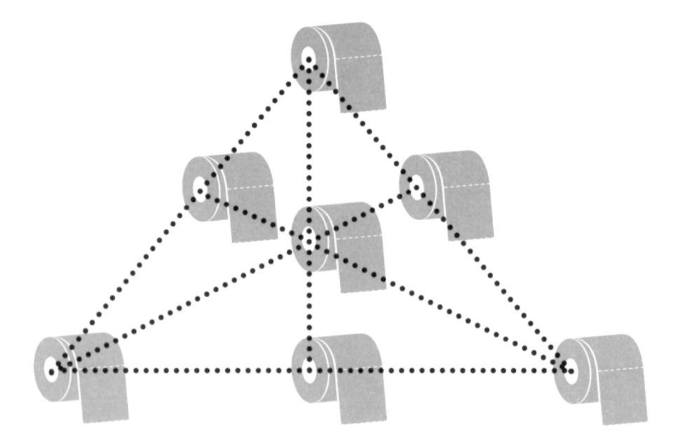

2. One - after that it is not empty.

3.

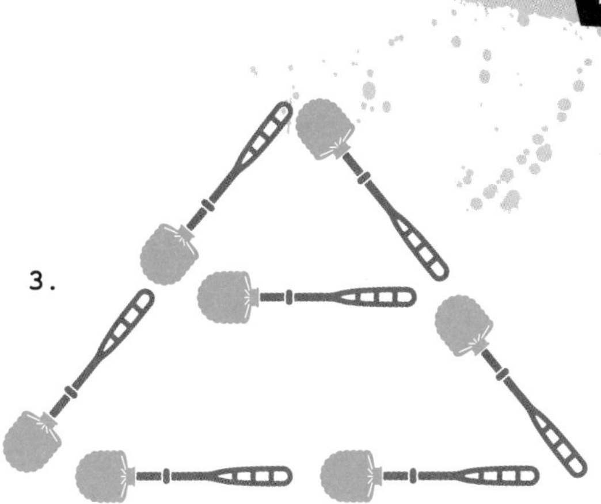

4. It would take Den 240 minutes. Here's why:

If it takes Len 120 minutes to do it all, then in the 80 minutes they work together, he is doing ⅔ of the job. That means Den is doing ⅓ of the work in the 80 minutes. 80 minutes times 3 is 240 minutes.

5. None – it's a hole.

6. 20. No trick here, it's just 20!

7. Of course she can use the loo. She has a 10p and a 20p – *one* of them is not a 10 pence piece.

8. He can do it in 2. Here's how:

Jeff would need to divide the pills into three sets of three. Using his scales he can compare one set of three against one other set of three.

If they don't balance, then Jeff can see which set has a lighter pill – he needs to pick this set and ignore the others.

If they balance, both those sets can be set aside and he should pick the three pills he hasn't weighed yet.

Either way, he should now have three pills left. He can pick any two and compare one against another. He now knows that the lightest pill on the scales must be his laxative, or if they balance, it is the one he didn't weigh.

Easy! Ahem...

9. Here are the answers for question 9. Your answer could be a mirror image or a rotated version – it's still the same answer!

If you found others, then well done, you can tell your friends that you are king of the loo brush!

a. b.

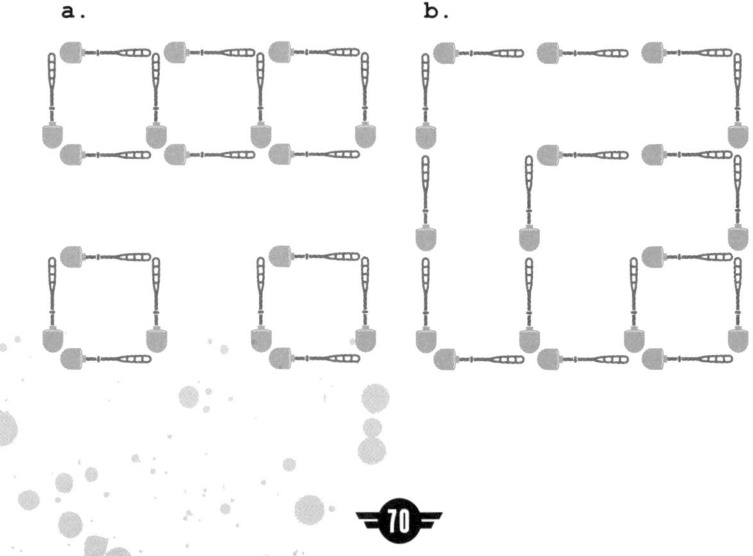

c.

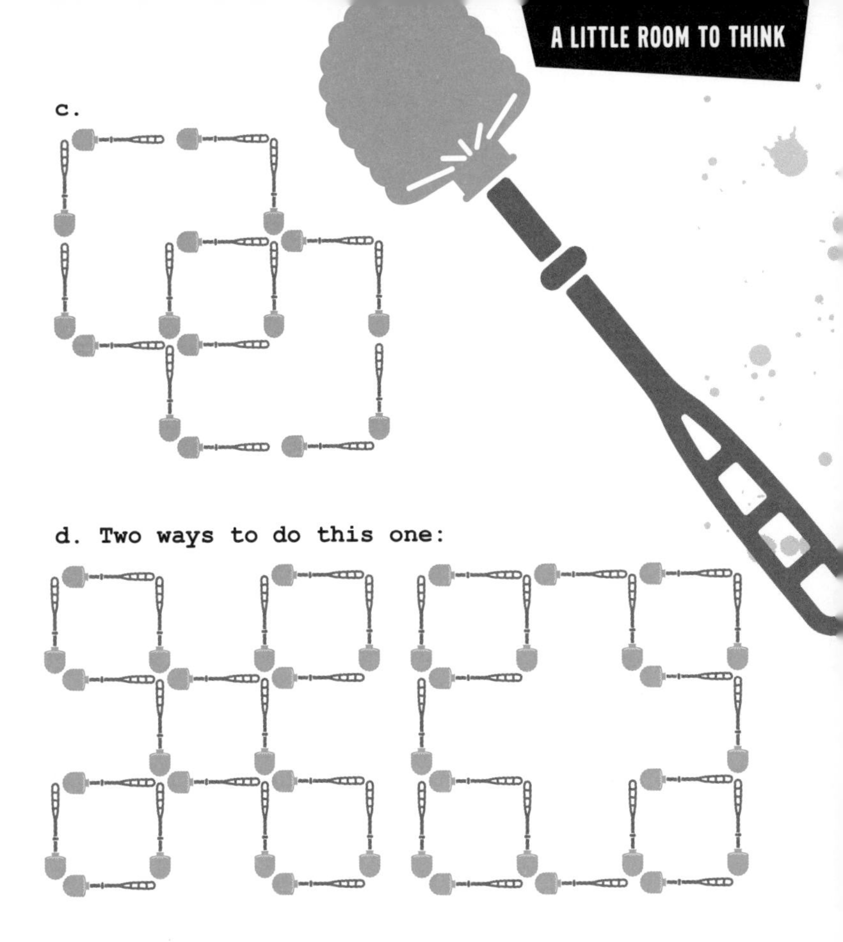

d. Two ways to do this one:

10. The toilet roll holder was £10.50 and the roll was 50p. If you were thinking £10 and £1, they are £9 different...

# ON THE RUNS

"I've never had a problem with drugs.
I've had problems with the police."

*Keith Richards*

The last thing you want to be when stopped by the police is a comedian. You should be safe where you are – the long arm of the law doesn't reach under the toilet door. Here are a few cautionary tales for the next time you are caught short.

# Animal House

**** ****

**A burglar broke into a house one night.**

He shone his torch around, looking for valuables, and when he picked up an iPod, a strange, disembodied voice echoed from the dark saying, "Jesus is watching you." He nearly jumped out of his skin, clicked off his torch and froze.

After a bit, when he heard nothing more, he shook his head, clicked the light back on and began searching for more valuables. Just as he pulled the stereo out so he could disconnect the wires, clear as a bell he heard, **"Jesus is watching you."** Freaked out, he shone his light around frantically, looking for the source of the voice. Finally, in the corner of the room, his torch beam came to rest on a parrot.

"Did you say that?" he hissed at the parrot.

**"Yep," the parrot confessed, "I'm just trying to warn you."**

The burglar relaxed. "Warn me, huh? Who the hell are you?"

"Moses," replied the bird.

"Moses?" the burglar laughed. "What kind of stupid people would name a parrot Moses?"

"Probably the same kind of people that would name a Rottweiler Jesus," the bird answered.

# That's Admiral, OH YES

Crap 'O' Matic

A few choice phrases from genuine insurance claim forms:

- Coming home I drove into the wrong house and collided with a tree I don't have.
- I thought my window was down, but I found it was up when I put my head through it.
- I collided with a stationary truck coming the other way.
- The guy was all over the road. I had to swerve a number of times before I hit him.
- I pulled away from the side of the road, glanced at my mother-in-law and headed over the embankment.
- In an attempt to kill a fly I drove into a telephone pole.
- I had been driving for forty years when I fell asleep at the wheel and had an accident.
- My car was legally parked as it backed into another vehicle.
- An invisible car came out of nowhere, struck my car and vanished.
- I saw a slow-moving, sad-faced old gentleman as he bounced off the roof of my car.
- I was thrown from my car as it left the road. I was later found in a ditch by some stray cows.

## Guilty As Charged

A woman was caught stealing a can of peaches from her local supermarket. When her trial began, her husband watched from the public gallery.

"How many peaches were in the can?" asked the judge.

"Six," she confessed.

"Then I must sentence you to six years in prison, one for every peach you stole," said the judge.

Her husband stood up and said, "Judge. She also stole a bag of peas."

## **** EVENING AL ****

A policeman working nights was relieved of duty early and arrived home at 3am.

Not wanting to wake his wife, he undressed in the dark, crept into the bedroom and started to climb into bed.

She sleepily sat up and said, "Alan, would you pop out to the 24-hour chemist and get me some aspirin? I've got a splitting headache."

"Of course, love," he said, and feeling his way across the room, he got dressed and went to the chemist that was on his usual beat.

As he arrived, the pharmacist looked up in surprise. "Hi Alan. I thought you were a copper?"

"I am," said Alan.

"Well then, why the hell are you wearing a fireman's uniform?"

Plop-O-Matic

## I Need Answers

A man went to the police station demanding to talk to the burglar who had broken into his house the night before.

"You'll get your chance in court," said the desk sergeant.

"No, no, no!" said the man. "I want to know how he got into the house without waking my wife. I've been trying to do that for years!"

**WHAT DID THE POLICEMAN SAY TO HIS BELLY BUTTON?**

**YOU'RE UNDER A VEST!**

## Theft Identity

A bank robber was about to make his getaway when he asked one of his hostages, "Did you see my face?"

The man replied "Yes", and the robber shot him dead.

He asked a female hostage, "Did you see my face?"

"No," she said, "but I think my husband did."

# Duncan Disorderly

A policeman pulled over a driver who had been weaving all over the road. He said to the driver, "Sir, I need you to blow into this breathalyser tube."

The driver said, "Sorry officer, I can't do that. I am an asthmatic. If I do that I'll have a really bad asthma attack."

"Okay, fine. I need you to come down to the station to give a blood sample."

"I can't do that either. I am a haemophiliac. If I do that, I'll bleed to death."

"Well, then we need a urine sample."

"I'm sorry officer, I can't do that either. I am also a diabetic. If I do that I'll get really low blood sugar."

"All right then, I need you to come out here and walk on this white line."

"I can't do that, officer."

"Why not?"

"Because I'm way too drunk."

**A POLICE OFFICER CAME UP TO ME YESTERDAY AND SAID, "WHERE WERE YOU BETWEEN FOUR AND SIX?"**

**I REPLIED, "PRIMARY SCHOOL."**

## Lost

**** ****

A woman, crying her heart out, went up to a policeman. She told him that she had lost her little dog, Benji.

The policeman suggested she put up some posters or put an ad in the paper.

"That's no good," she replied, "Benji can't read."

## Doctor The Evidence

A lawyer was cross-examining a doctor. "Before you signed the death certificate had you taken the man's pulse?"

"No," the doctor replied.

"Well then, did you listen for a heartbeat?"

The doctor answered, "No."

"Did you check for respiration? Breathing?" asked the lawyer.

Again the doctor replied, "No."

"Ah," the lawyer said. "So when you signed the death certificate you had not taken any steps to make sure the man was dead, had you?"

The doctor rolled his eyes, and said, "At the time I signed the death certificate the man's brain was sitting in a jar on my desk. But I can see your point. For all I know he could be out there practising law somewhere."

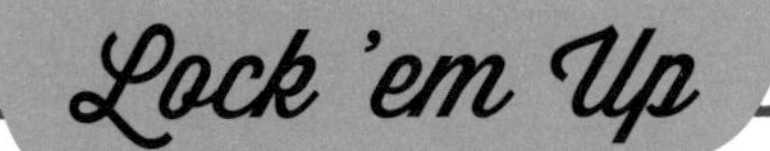

## Lock 'em Up

Some children were on a field trip to a police station. A policeman was showing them around and talking about how to stay out of trouble.

Little Johnny saw a set of Wanted posters on the wall and asked, "Are you really trying to catch all of those men?"

"Yes," replied the policeman, happy that someone was taking an interest.

"Well," little Johnny continued, "why didn't you lock them up when you took their photographs?"

## **** MEDIA SOLUTION ****

A woman went to the police station to report her husband missing after he didn't come home for a few days. The desk sergeant took down the details and took a good look at the photo she provided.

"We will most likely ask the local media to help with this," said the sergeant. "Is there any message you would like to get to him?"

"Yes," she replied. "Tell him Mother didn't come after all."

# TUSK, TUSK

A jeweller called the police station to report a robbery. "A truck backed up to my store, the doors opened and an elephant came out. He broke my plate-glass window, stuck his trunk in, sucked up all my necklaces and climbed back into the truck. The doors closed and the truck pulled away."

The desk sergeant said, "Could you tell me, for identification purposes, whether it was an Indian elephant or an African elephant?"

"What's the difference?" asked the jeweller.

"Well," said the sergeant, "an African elephant has great big ears and an Indian elephant has little ears."

"Come to think of it, I couldn't see his ears," said the jeweller. "He had a stocking over his head."

# Good Will Hunting

A man asked his lawyer how he should go about drawing up a will.

The lawyer said, "No problem, leave it all to me."

The man, somewhat taken aback, said, "I know you want a percentage, but leave something for my wife and kids."

**WHY ARE LAWYERS BANNED FROM HAVING SEX WITH THEIR CLIENTS?**

**SO THE CLIENT CAN'T BE BILLED TWICE FOR THE SAME SERVICE.**

Crap 'O' Matic

## *Limericks*

### A FEW LEGAL RHYMES THAT ARE COMPLETELY LAWFUL...

A streaker was in court, appealing
His sentence too high, near the ceiling
"I ask you, your grace
To review my case
The details are very revealing"

The police found the lab in a state
With nitrogen stolen so late
In securing the site
They'd work through the night
And be paid on a copper nitrate

There was once a policeman called Pete
Who was always asleep on the beat
It was hard to keep pace
When the burglar gave chase
So he just had arrest in the street

"A computer once beat me at chess, but it was no match for me at kick boxing."

*Emo Philips*

You can't stop progress, but you can pretend it's not happening for five minutes when you are in the smallest room. Computers, unemployment, tax, insurance, celebrity culture and the internet are all part of our everyday lives whether we like it or not. At least we can still have a laugh while we download.

## Know-it-all

A computer salesman is trying to sell a customer a new computer that can answer absolutely any question. The customer is intrigued, but wants a demo before going any further.

The customer asks the computer where his mother is. After a few seconds the computer responds, "Your mother is staying with her sister in Exeter." The customer is amazed that the computer is right.

The salesman seizes the moment and makes the sale. As he is preparing to leave, the customer has another go on the computer and asks where his father is. It responds with, "Your father is in New York on a business trip."

"Hold on a minute," says the customer, "that's rubbish. My father has been dead for two years."

The computer hears this and immediately comes back with, "No, the man your mother married has been dead for two years. Your father is on a business trip in New York."

**I WAS IN A QUEUE FOR A CASHPOINT YESTERDAY WHEN THIS LITTLE OLD LADY ASKED IF I COULD HELP CHECK HER BALANCE. SO I PUSHED HER OVER.**

* * * *

## First Class

A young man reported for his first day of work at the supermarket. The manager greeted him with a warm handshake and a smile, handed him a broom and said, "Right, your first job is to sweep out the fruit and veg aisle."

"But I've just graduated from university," the young man replied indignantly.

"Oh, I'm sorry, I didn't realise," said the manager. "Here, give me the broom - I'll show you how."

## Invention

Michelle and Kate were on a girls' night out at the pub. They fancied a smoke so had to go outside. Unfortunately, it started to rain. Michelle looked in her handbag, pulled out a condom, cut off the end, put it over her cigarette and continued smoking.

Kate asked, "What are you doing?"

Michelle replied, "Oh, it's a condom. This way my cigarette doesn't get wet."

Kate liked the idea so the following day she went to her local shop and asked for a box of condoms. The shop assistant asked what brand she wanted.

Kate replied, "It doesn't matter as long as it fits a Camel."

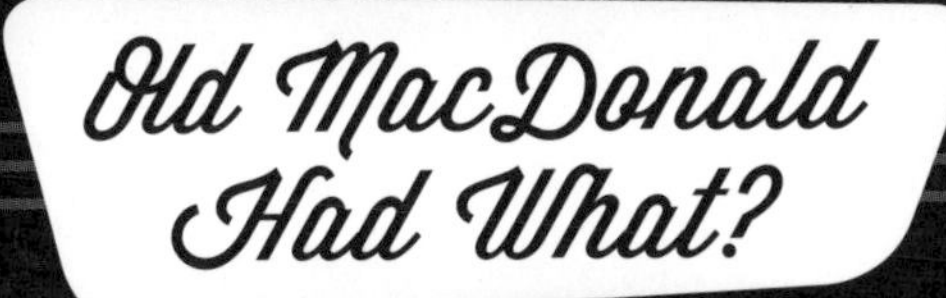


A group of young children were sitting in a circle with their teacher. She was going around in turn asking them all questions.

"David, what noise does a cow make?"

"It goes moo, miss."

"Alice, what noise does a cat make?"

"It goes meow, miss."

"James, what sound does a lamb make?"

"It goes baaa, miss."

"Jenny, what sound does a mouse make?"

"Errr... it goes... click...?"

**** ****

There was once a man who, in his youth, professed his desire to become a great writer.

When asked to define "great" he said, "I want to write stuff that the whole world will read, stuff that people will react to on a truly emotional level, stuff that will make them scream, cry, howl in pain and anger!"

He now works for Microsoft, writing error messages.

## Like For Like

Diana's car was stolen so she called the insurance company and said, "I had that car insured for fifteen thousand – I want my money!"

The agent replied, "Sorry madam, insurance doesn't work quite like that. An independent adjuster will assess the value of what was insured, and then we'll provide you with another car, just like the original one."

There was a long pause, and then Diana replied, "If that's how it works, I want to cancel the life insurance policy on my husband."

## Turn It Up To Eleven

Dave was out and about when he realised he really needed to fart. The music was so loud he thought he might be able to hide the noise if he let it out to the beat.

When the rowdy chorus kicked in he farted a little bit on each beat and let off one final blow when the tune reached its climax.

Happy with his work, he wondered why everyone else stopped what they were doing and started staring at him.

Then Dave remembered he was listening to his iPod.

## EINSTEIN DEVELOPED A THEORY ABOUT SPACE, AND IT WAS ABOUT TIME TOO.

**** Limericks ****

### MODERN LIFE IN A MAD METER...

As my laptop was somewhat forlorn
My son took it, and fixed it, with scorn
When he gave it back
It seemed sharp as a tack
But the hard drive was packed full of porn

There came a "ring ring" on my phone
On the screen it said "caller unknown"
I hung up the line
As my gas company's fine
And I don't need more texts or a loan

The incredible Wizard of Oz
Retired from his business becoz
Due to up-to-date science
To most of his clients
He wasn't the wizard he woz

## AFTER YEARS OF TRYING, I MANAGED TO INSERT HUMAN DNA INTO A GOAT. NOW I'M BANNED FROM THE PETTING ZOO.

# Can We FIX IT?

The internet makes it much easier and quicker to complain.

Be careful though – consider your words carefully before you fire off that email or tweet. These folks didn't when they contacted their local council:

- It's the dogs' mess that I find hard to swallow.
- I want some repairs done to my cooker as it has backfired and burnt my knob off.
- Their 18-year-old son is continually banging his balls against my fence.
- I wish to report that tiles are missing from the outside toilet roof. I think it was bad wind the other night that blew them off.
- My lavatory seat is cracked, where do I stand?
- I am writing on behalf of my sink, which is coming away from the wall.
- Will you please send someone to mend the garden path. My wife tripped and fell on it yesterday and now she is pregnant.
- I request permission to remove my drawers in the kitchen.
- 50% of the walls are damp, 50% have crumbling plaster and 50% are plain filthy.

- The toilet is blocked and we cannot bath the children until it is cleared.
- Our lavatory seat is broken in half and is now in three pieces.
- The man next door has a large erection in the back garden, which is unsightly and dangerous.
- I am a single woman living in a downstairs flat and would you please do something about the noise made by the man on top of me every night.
- This is to let you know that our lavatory seat is broke and we can't get BBC2.

## **** WHAT'S IN A NAME? ****

The wife and I were overjoyed when our new baby arrived. I walked proudly into the registry office and said, "We'd like to call her Sarah."

"Sorry," said the registrar. "Sarah has already been assigned. You might like Sarah1625 or Sarah_baby_17."

**I WAS WATCHING THE LONDON MARATHON AND SAW ONE RUNNER DRESSED AS A CHICKEN AND ANOTHER RUNNER DRESSED AS AN EGG. I THOUGHT: "THIS COULD BE INTERESTING..."**

ENGAGED

## Pinch To Zoom

My wife grabbed my new phone and shouted, "You're obsessed with this bloody thing. It gets more attention than me, I'm gonna throw it against the bloody wall!"

"Wait!" I shouted. "At least let me put it in flight mode first."

****

**EBAY ITEM DESCRIPTION: PARACHUTE. ONLY USED ONCE, NEVER OPENED, SMALL STAIN.**

****

## Memorable Phrase

A wife was helping her husband set up a new email account. Halfway through, she told him that he would need to enter a password.

The husband was in a cheeky mood and thought he would try to make his wife laugh. When the computer asked him to enter his password, he made it plainly obvious to his wife that he was keying in "penis".

She certainly did start laughing as the computer replied, "Password rejected: not long enough."

## I CAN'T BELIEVE HOW MUCH MONEY THIS MOBILE PHONE IS COSTING ME. EVERY TIME I PLUG IT IN, IT TELLS ME IT'S CHARGING.

## Anne Owed Too Tie-Pose

Eye halve a spelling chequer
It came with my pea sea
It plainly marques four my revue
Miss steaks eye kin knot sea.

Eye strike a quay and type a word
And weight four it two say
Weather eye am wrong oar write
It shows me strait a weigh.

As soon as a mist ache is maid
It nose bee fore two long
And eye can put the error rite
It's rare lea ever wrong.

Eye have run this poem threw it
I am shore your pleased two no
It's letter perfect awl the weigh
My chequer tolled me sew.

*(Attributed to Martha Snow)*

Pull FOR Flush

**YOUNGSTERS SEEM SO OBSESSED WITH FAME THESE DAYS. "LIFE ISN'T ALL ABOUT QUICK STARDOM AND AWARDS CEREMONIES," IS WHAT I TOLD MY KIDS, OSCAR, EMMY AND BRIT.**

## Return To Sender

Phil arrived in the South of France for a well-deserved holiday. Unfortunately, due to work problems, his wife Emma couldn't join him until the following day. Once checked into the hotel, Phil sent Emma an email to let her know all was OK.

But Phil was not the best with technology and he got her email address wrong. He accidentally sent the email to a complete stranger - an old lady who had been to her husband's funeral just the day before.

She opened the email and fainted immediately on reading it. Thankfully, her daughter was staying with her so she quickly helped her come round and comforted her. The daughter wondered what caused the sudden panic so she read the email:

"Darling, got here safely. Looking forward to your arrival tomorrow. Just so you know, it's REALLY hot down here!"

# Smile Please

A man was driving when he saw the flash of a traffic camera. He wondered why as he was sure he wasn't speeding.

Just to check, he went around the block and passed the same spot, driving even more slowly, but again the camera flashed.

Now he began to think that this was quite funny, so he drove even slower as he passed the area again, but the traffic camera again flashed.

He tried a fourth time with the same result. He did this a fifth time and was now laughing when the camera flashed as he rolled past, this time at a snail's pace.

Two weeks later, he got five summonses in the post for driving without a seat belt.

****

A SCIENTIST KEPT TELLING MILDLY RACIST JOKES WHILE HE PERFORMED HIS EXPERIMENTS.

HE ONLY DID IT TO GET A REACTION.

****

Some genuine news stories, straight from the loo papers:

## QUESTIONS IN THE HOUSE

The Houses of Parliament ran out of toilet paper recently and it was all down to the KGB. No, not that KGB but KGB Cleaning Supplies who failed to deliver enough paper to satisfy the MPs and Peers. It is not known whether they resorted to using copies of the Prime Minister's speech.

## IN SPACE, NO ONE CAN HEAR YOU SCREAM

Russian cosmonauts on the International Space Station were banned from using the US-installed toilets after bureaucrats argued over funding issues. The Russians retaliated by no longer sharing their food – unsurprisingly, this had no effect on negotiations.

## HOSED

Australian firefighters attending a blaze in New South Wales were not best pleased when they were assisted by a water-bombing helicopter. Rather than filling up from the local reservoir, it accidentally collected water from a sewage treatment plant. Thankfully, the firefighters managed to put the fire out and suffered no ill-effects. There is no news of what they did to the helicopter pilot...

## ON THREE...

Authorities in Bulawayo, Zimbabwe, asked the city's residents to join in a "synchronised flush" to help clear the sewers. Water is rationed in Bulawayo so the sewers get clogged easily. They hope to make the event regular.

## IN CASE OF EMERGENCY

Devon and Cornwall police received an emergency call from a man who had "run out of toilet paper". This was one of many frivolous calls they received on the 999 number in 2012, including reports of "a leak in the bathroom" and "the Chinese takeaway is not answering the phone".

This edition published by Parragon Books Ltd in 2014

Parragon Books Ltd
Chartist House
15–17 Trim Street
Bath BA1 1HA, UK
www.parragon.com



Written by Roffy
Packaged by: Susanna Geoghegan Gift Publishing
Interior layout: Seagull Design



ISBN 978-1-4723-7113-3

Printed in China